MARSHES & SWAMPS

By Gail Gibbons

Holiday House   New York

Special thanks to Mike Owen of the Fakahatchee Strand State Preserve, Copeland, Florida.

To the kids of the Everglades City School, Florida

Library of Congress Cataloging-in-Publication Data
Gibbons, Gail.
    Marshes and swamps / by Gail Gibbons.
       p.   cm.
    Summary: Defines marshes and swamps, discusses how conditions in
them may change, and examines the life found in and around them.
    ISBN 0-8234-1347-0
    1. Marshes—Juvenile literature.   2. Swamps—Juvenile literature.
[1. Marshes. 2. Swamps.]   I. Title.
GB621.G53   1998   97-17995   CIP   AC
551.41—dc21

  ISBN-13: 978-0-8234-1347-8 (hardcover)
  ISBN-13: 978-0-8234-1515-1 (paperback)

  ISBN-10: 0-8234-1347-0 (hardcover)
  ISBN-10: 0-8234-1515-5 (paperback)

WETLAND

MUD is wet SOIL

Marshes and swamps are wetlands. They are made up of soaked, wet ground or are covered with shallow water over a muddy bottom. From the mud, plants take root to send their stems, leaves and flowers up above the water.

MARSH

A marsh is made up of many grassy plants and sometimes a few shrubs. There are no trees or woody plants.

SWAMP

Swamps have trees, bushes and shrubs. Most swamps began as marshes when dead plants began to pile up and decay. In the marsh, more mud was made. As the area became shallower, trees, bushes and shrubs took root in the mud. They grew to cover much of the marshy area which then became a swamp.

TUNDRA

DESERT MARSH

Wetlands are found throughout the world. Some of today's wetlands have existed for about 10,000 years. In the tundra of the far North, marshes form when frozen ground thaws and melts. Sometimes desert marshes form near a spring of water.

Marshes and swamps are found in open, wide lowlands, along seacoasts, and around ponds, lakes and riverbeds.

Marshes and swamps have different kinds of water. Some have fresh water, and some have saltwater. Others are a mixture of fresh water and saltwater. This happens when ocean water mixes with fresh water from ponds, lakes and rivers.

FRESHWATER MARSHES

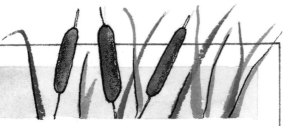

Freshwater marshes form around the edges of lakes, rivers and ponds. Some are no bigger than a few feet across. Others are huge . . . as far as you can see! The Everglades, in Florida, is the biggest freshwater marsh in the world. It is about 4,000 square miles.

RED-WINGED BLACKBIRD

DEER

CATTAILS

REEDS

BEAVER

DRAGONFLY

SPOTTED TURTLE

MUSKRAT

WATER SNAKE

GOLDEN SHINERS

A freshwater marsh is made up of grassy plants such as reeds, cattails, duckweed and rushes. It is an ideal place for insects to live.

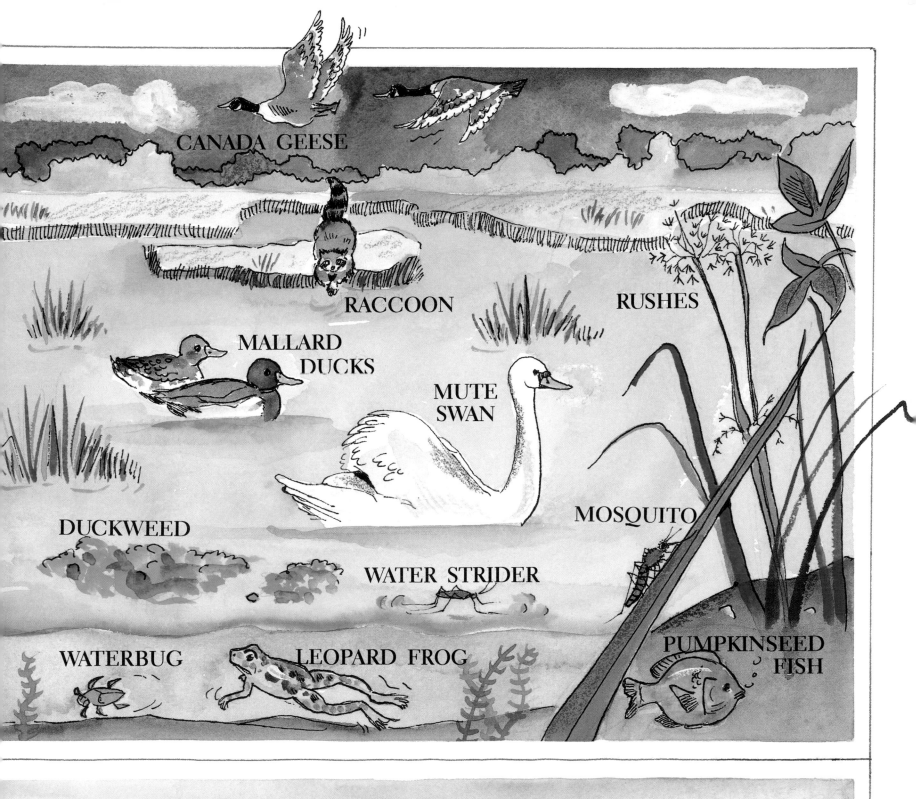

Many different kinds of fish, birds and other animals are able
to live in this kind of environment.

SALTWATER MARSHES

HIGH TIDE

AMERICAN AVOCET

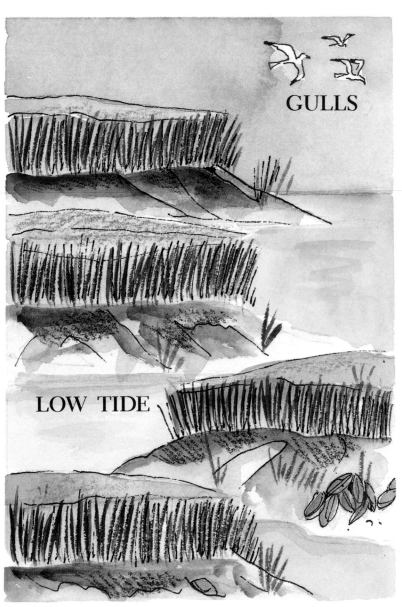

GULLS

LOW TIDE

Saltwater marshes are found along coastlines. Tides create the water level. At high tide a large part of the saltwater marsh is under water. During low tide much of the land is visible.

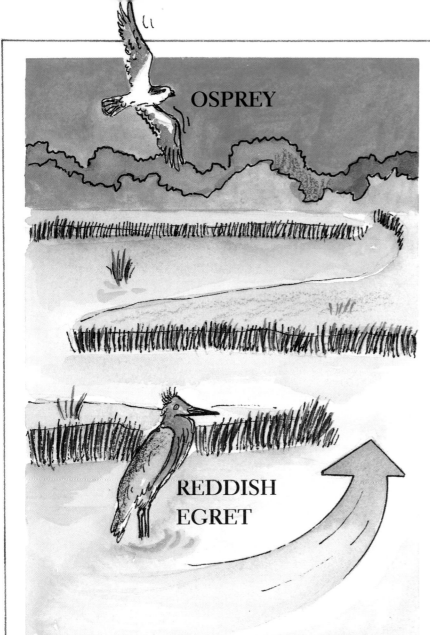

OSPREY

REDDISH
EGRET

SANDPIPERS

When the tide rises and enters a saltwater marsh, it brings saltwater to the marsh, creating a rich, growing place for the plants and creatures living there. When the tide reverses and the saltwater drains back out to sea, it carries bits of dead plants and animals that become food for the fish that live in the ocean.

RING-BILLED GULL

OSPREY

BROWN PELICAN

SNOWY EGRET

OPOSSUM

FLOUNDER

MOSQUITO FISH

In the United States most saltwater marshes are found along the East Coast and the Gulf of Mexico. That's because there is a lot of flat, low land near the shores. Saltwater marshes teem with life.

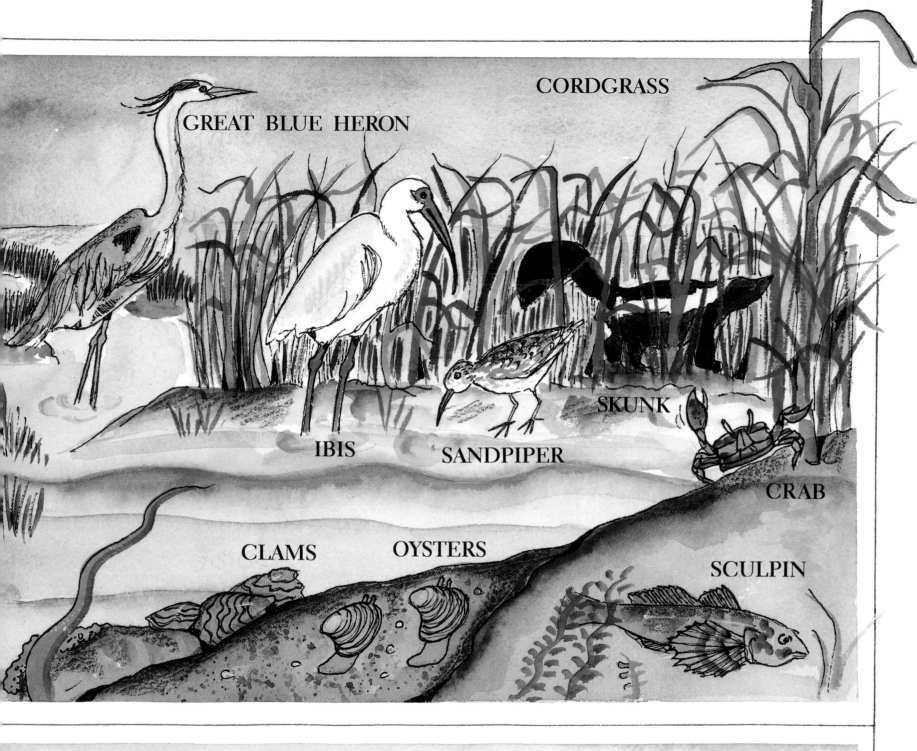

GREAT BLUE HERON

CORDGRASS

IBIS

SANDPIPER

SKUNK

CRAB

CLAMS

OYSTERS

SCULPIN

The plants, fish and animals that live there have adapted to the daily rising and falling of the water.

FRESHWATER SWAMPS

WOODPECKER

DEER

BOBCAT

BEAR

BUCK MOTH

Freshwater swamps are always waterlogged. The water levels change with the amounts of rainfall they receive. The trees and other plants will live as long as their roots aren't under water for long periods of time.

SILVER MAPLE

ASH

MOOSE

WILLOW

BEAVER

ARROWHEAD

TOAD

Different kinds of plants and animals are found in different swamp locations. In cooler swamps one might find silver maple, willow and ash trees growing. Often, moose come to feed on swamp plants. There is a lot of wildlife.

RED
MAPLE

BOBCAT

An
EPIPHYTE
is also called
an AIR
PLANT.

PANTHER

WOOD
STORK

BALD
CYPRESS
TREE

WATER HYACINTH

COTTONMOUTH
SNAKE

EGRET

SNAPPING TURTLE

DUCKWEED

LONG-NOSED GAR

In some warm climates the bald cypress tree grows. Its big base helps to hold it up out of the muddy bottom. Its special roots have stumpy shapes, called knees, that stick out of the water.

BARRED OWL

SPANISH MOSS

OTTERS

ALLIGATOR

CYPRESS KNEE

BULLFROG

CRAYFISH

This is often a dark, damp wetland. All kinds of sounds are heard. A barred owl screeches. An alligator slaps the water. A bullfrog croaks. Birds peck at the mud and water for their food.

MANGROVE SWAMPS

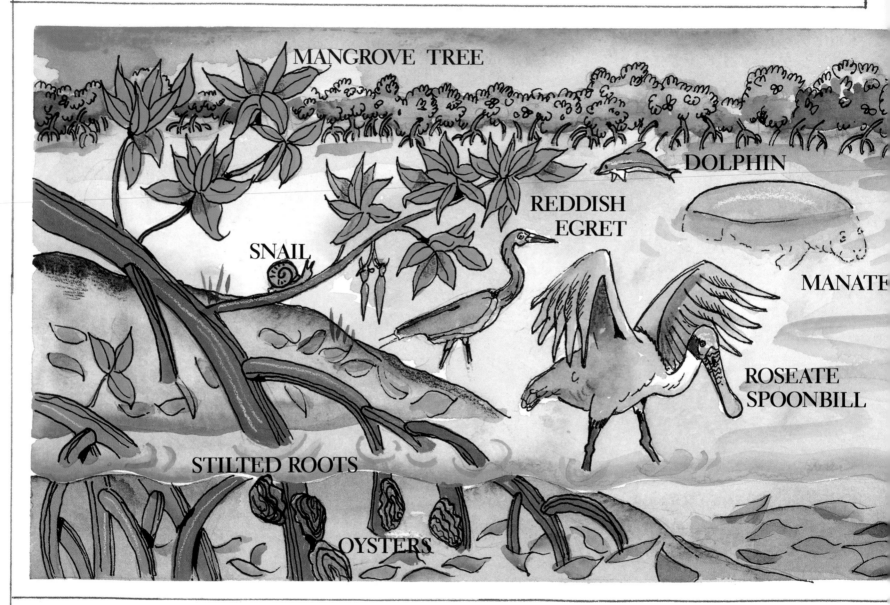

MANGROVE TREE

DOLPHIN

REDDISH EGRET

SNAIL

MANATEE

ROSEATE SPOONBILL

STILTED ROOTS

OYSTERS

Mangrove swamps have a mixture of saltwater and fresh water. They are found along tropical seacoasts. Mangrove swamps are named after the mangrove trees that grow there. These trees stand above the water on roots that look like stilts.

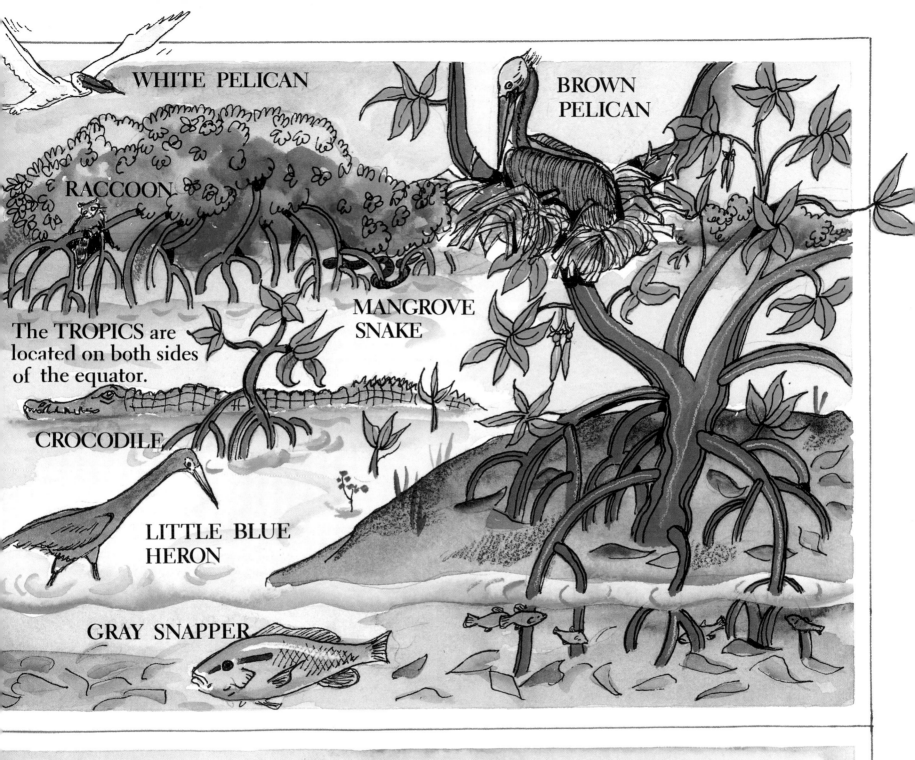

WHITE PELICAN

BROWN PELICAN

RACCOON

MANGROVE SNAKE

The TROPICS are located on both sides of the equator.

CROCODILE

LITTLE BLUE HERON

GRAY SNAPPER

These tangled roots are shelter for the many creatures that live there. Small fish swim around the roots. In big branches, brown pelicans make their nests.

IBIS

ROSEATE SPOONBILL

MANGROVE TERRAPIN

SEA HORSE

CRAB

Mangrove trees allow land to form. When dead plants and mud collect around a mangrove tree's roots, soil builds up. Bit by bit an island begins to take shape. It will become home for other plants and animals.

Each marsh and swamp is an ecosystem, which is a place where plants and animals interact as a natural unit.

EROSION is the wearing away of soil by water.

Marshes and swamps are vital storage places for one of Earth's most precious resources, water. While storing large amounts of water, these areas reduce the chance of flooding in other places. Also, their plant life helps to stop the erosion of the surrounding land.

Many kinds of plants and animals need wetlands to survive. When wetlands are filled with dirt to create more land to build on, they are destroyed forever. Many acres of marshes and swamps have already been destroyed.

When marshes and swamps disappear, so do countless numbers of plants and animals. Many people are working to save our wetlands from destruction.

In some places boardwalks have been built over marshes and through swamps. That way people can walk into the natural beauty of swamps and marshes without disturbing the plants and animals that live there.

Marshes and swamps are wonderful places to explore. They have some of the most unusual landscapes in the world. They are home to many interesting creatures.

Many of these strange and beautiful places have been made refuges and preserves to protect their unusual plant and animal life. For the visitor they are always full of surprises.

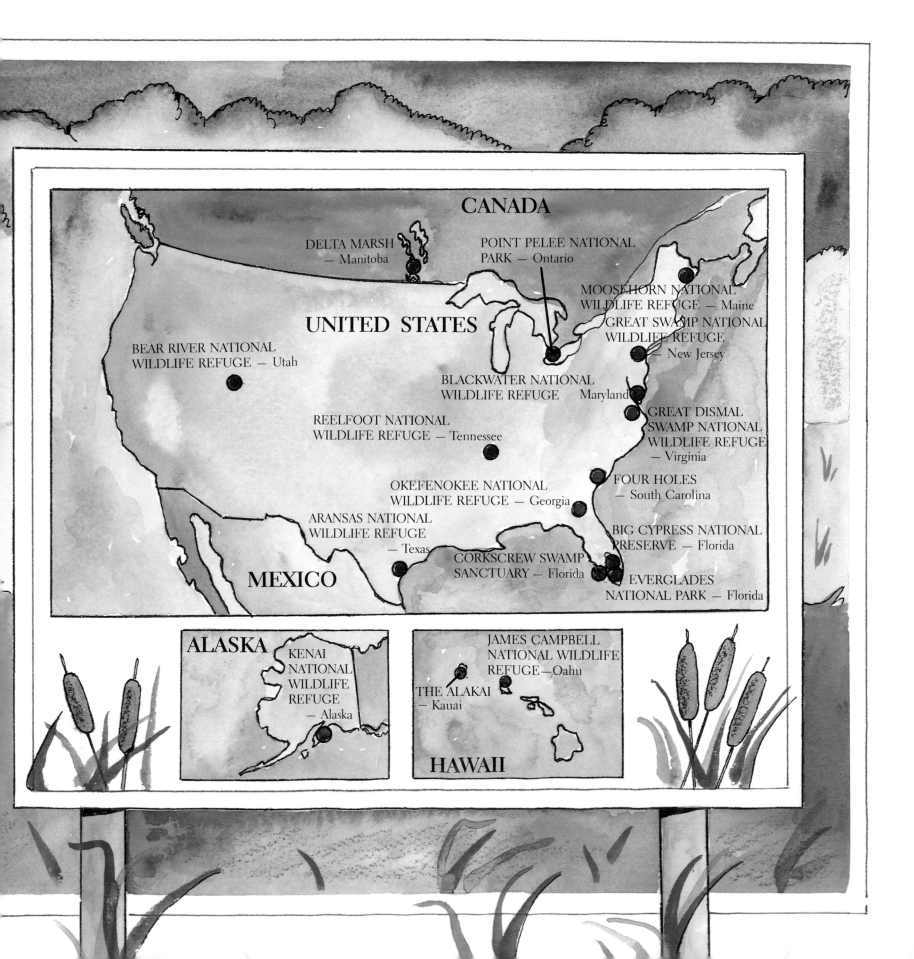

MORE ABOUT WETLANDS

The first wetlands formed about 300 million years ago.

Two-thirds of all wetland areas in the United States are found in Alaska.

Wetlands make up six percent of Earth's land areas.

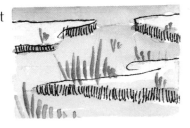

Africa has more wetlands than any other continent.

A bog is a wetland, too. Bogs are spongy, mossy wetlands where dead plants pile up faster than they can rot away. Walking on a bog feels like walking on a mattress. Each step seems to shake the whole bog.

Sections of some big cities were built where wetlands used to be. These include Boston, San Francisco and Washington, D.C.

Some scientists believe that more than one-third of the endangered and threatened animals and plants in the United States depend on wetlands to survive.

Marshes and swamps are important stopovers for migrating birds.

Less than half of the 215 million acres of wetlands that were in the continental United States still exist.